SIMPLE STRATEGIES FOR THE BAR EXAM

Practical tips and tactics to help you face the
bar exam with confidence

WILL LOWREY

SIMPLE STRATEGIES FOR THE BAR EXAM
Copyright © 2019 by William C. Lowrey

This book is not intended as a substitute for robust bar preparation and materials. The purpose of this book is only to serve as a supplement to comprehensive bar preparation. The author makes no guarantees that anyone following the tips, suggestions, tactics, and approaches contained in this book will pass the bar exam. The author bears no responsibility or liability with respect to any loss, damage, or alleged damage caused directly or indirectly by information contained in this book.

The author is not engaged in rendering legal or other professional advice, and this publication is not a substitute for the advice of an attorney. If you require legal or other expert advice, you should seek the services of a competent attorney or other professional.

Editing by Lana Mowdy
Cover Design by Pixel Studio
Formatting by The Book Khaleesi

ISBN 978-1-7329399-4-3 (e-book)

Published by Lomack Publishing
www.lomackpublising.com

LOMACK
PUBLISHING

First Edition

TABLE OF CONTENTS

DISCLAIMERS

This book is NOT intended as a complete study guide for the bar exam.

This book does not replace traditional bar preparation materials. It merely supplements these materials with suggestions and approaches that have proven useful to the author.

The author makes no warranties whatsoever regarding the reader's likelihood to pass the bar exam upon the completion of any portion of this book.

This book provides general guidance regarding the bar exam and DOES NOT intend to provide specific jurisdictional rules and requirements.

Readers MUST consult their specific jurisdictional rules to understand the components of their individual tests, the rules of the examination, and any procedural requirements.

But you knew all that already, so let's get on with it.

To Ripley — my crippled little dog, who never gives up.

CHAPTER ONE

Introduction

The Bar Exam.

Those three simple words strike fear in the heart of every law student approaching graduation. Throughout law school, you've probably heard these words dozens, if not hundreds, of times from classmates, faculty, friends, and coworkers at your internships. Invariably, when these words are spoken, they are uttered with something of a dreadful reverence. People speak these words as if conjuring the name of some long forgotten Cthulhu-like wraith that rises twice a year to torment sacrificial law students along their voyage to becoming an attorney. Based on all this, you've probably internalized that the bar exam is some beastly, terrifying spectacle that you must somehow muster the courage to vanquish in mortal combat in your pursuit of a legal career.

But, it doesn't have to be like that. It shouldn't be like that.

As you begin your journey towards the bar exam, I implore you to pause for a moment and put all the hype and nonsense you've heard off to the side. Take a critical look at the bar exam. Stare it in the face for what it is. The bar exam is not some nameless, faceless beast. When you accept the bar exam for what it is and dismiss all the accompanying hysteria, you will come to find that the bar exam is essentially just another boring test.

At its core, the bar exam is a couple dozen sheets of paper printed with questions and information that looks generally indistinguishable from dozens of other tests you've taken over your lifetime. Somewhere, months before, in some bland office, a group of perfectly normal human beings brainstormed and came up with the questions you will be asked to answer. They weren't witches gathered in a coven or sorcerers rubbing at some magical stone. They were just normal people, who were most likely in your shoes at some point. After they came up with these questions, someone typed them up, sent them off to be printed, and then thousands of copies of test booklets appeared. There is no wraith. There is no mystery. The bar exam is pretty mundane when it comes down to it.

You've been through routines like this before. The bar exam will occur on a pre-determined set of dates, in conference rooms and auditoriums that look like any you've been in a hundred times in your life. You will sit in chairs just like others you've sat in a thousand times before. You will be given testing booklets that look like standardized testing booklets you have seen previously. You will be asked questions on a finite set of topics that you will know well in advance. In fact, there will not be one subject that you have not had an opportunity to prepare for in advance. The questions will be structured in a way you are intimately familiar with, based on hundreds of hours of preparation looking at questions exactly like the ones you will face on the bar exam. And in the end, you will reach into your mind and extract knowledge that lays ready to be retrieved and write or type it just as you have for hundreds of tests and quizzes throughout your years in school. And the odds say, if you put in the time, you will pass. Then you can forget all about the bar exam forever.

There is no question the bar exam is challenging and can be mentally and physically draining. But it absolutely does not have to be the dreaded rite of passage that it has been made to seem over the last three years of your life. Accept the bar exam for what it is but don't make it out to be something it isn't.

As a somewhat related side note, I have been a lifelong advocate for pit bull type dogs. It dawned on me at some point that the fear of the bar exam is a lot like the fear that people so often have about these dogs. With pit bull type dogs, the media and public have fueled a general perception that these dogs are monstrous, unpredictable, and something to be feared. So many people with limited exposure to these animals take these stories at face value and develop a deep phobia of these dogs. They'll cross the street when they see one coming, they'll read news propaganda about dog attacks and log mental notes about these dogs, and they will ultimately develop a foreboding, personal fear and distrust of something they have never actually experienced.

Invariably, however, when people actually expose themselves to a pit bull type dog and learn what they are all about, they change. They realize their fear existed because they let stories and anecdotes fill their mind and shape their beliefs and never really stopped to experience things for themselves. The bar exam is a lot like that. People fear the bar exam because it is new, it is unknown, and they have heard countless, awful stories about how brutal the exam is. Don't give in to the hysteria. Take a look at the bar exam in all its boring, drab, and monotonous glory and realize it is completely tangible, knowable, accessible, and most importantly – beatable. Once you put aside the hype, you've already taken one of the biggest steps towards passing the bar exam.

CHAPTER 2

Preparation

Without any question, the bar exam requires a significant amount of studying. "Significant" is probably an understatement. In fact, the vast majority of your time over the next several weeks and months will be spent with your nose in a book or laptop, consuming information in preparation for the bar exam.

But before you begin your studies in earnest, it is critical that you spend some time preparing to study. The bar exam is not an endeavor where you can just arbitrarily pick up a book, plop down in a chair, and start studying. Starting now, you should think of studying for the bar exam as a process – there is a defined start, end, and sequence of steps to get you there. The first step of this process is preparation. By preparing mentally, physically, and logistically before you begin, you will help ensure your actual study time is more efficient and productive.

1. Calibrate your mindset from the beginning

Before you begin, it is imperative you fully embrace and accept that studying for the bar exam is a slog. You must fully commit, without reservation. Studying for the bar exam is a long, brutal, grinding slog. There are no shortcuts. There are no secret formulas. Anyone who tells you otherwise is lying, got lucky, or most likely did not do very well on the exam. There is a direct correlation between time spent studying and bar passage rates. Every minute you spend trying to find a way to cut corners is a minute you avoided putting your head down and learning what you need to know.

It is absolutely essential that you are 150%

committed to this exam. This means you must realize and accept that the next 10-12 weeks of your life will largely be spent eating, sleeping, and breathing bar exam materials. If you find yourself thinking about how you can squeeze in a vacation, how you can keep up with your Friday night bar schedule, or how you can take on a part-time job, you are starting on the wrong foot.

Do people do these things and pass the bar exam? Sure. We've all had friends or acquaintances who passed the bar exam after taking extended vacations, enjoying Saturday nights at the club, or any myriad of other things. But why take this risk? Focusing on the bar exam above all else will substantially improve your odds of passing. Most people don't want to take the bar exam a second or third time. After you've finished studying for 10-12 weeks, the full weight of that truth will become evident. So, while it is theoretically possible to goof off and pass, it is simply not worth the risk in the long run, so don't even bother. The fact that you're even reading this book is a good sign you are committed to the process of studying. As such, you've already got an advantage on many others who will be taking the same exam. Hold on to that advantage.

In addition to commitment, you will need to find the time to study. Over the next 10-12 weeks, you should plan to spend anywhere from 40-60 hours a week studying. Studying for the bar exam is a full-time job and then some. This is not the time to take vacations, to enroll in evening pottery classes, or to pick up a new volunteer activity. You might find yourself studying 10 hours a day for 5 days a week or 8 hours a day for 7 days a week. The details are entirely up to you. Make a schedule that works, allocate the time, and stick to it. Your bar preparation program will undoubtedly have a calendar for you to follow. While those calendars may seem tedious and, at times, the activities may seem unnecessary, do not let yourself stray too far from the calendar. It is there for a reason and has been created and calibrated to maximize your chances for success.

As an example of one schedule (but by no means the only one), when I studied for my first and second bar exams, I would typically begin around 8:30am, study until 12:30pm, then take an extended break. I would view this lunchtime break as a reward for completing 4 hours of studying. During my break, I would eat lunch, walk the dogs, go to the gym, and run whatever errands absolutely needed to be done. Around 4:00pm, I would come back home to the computer and study until 9:00pm-10:00pm. My day was essentially broken into three components: (1) morning study period, (2) personal time, and (3) evening study period. Having that lengthy break in the middle of the day allowed me to handle the normal requirements of daily life, rest my mind for an extended period, and recharge a little before I went back to the computer. After the evening study period, I would wind down with an hour of surfing the internet or watching television and then get a good night's rest to repeat the process again the next day. I typically did this at least 6 days a week but, most of the time, 7 days a week. Your schedule may differ based on your personal situation, but the point of all this is that you should treat your studying like a full-time job. Create a study schedule that works for you based on your circumstances and stick to it religiously. Small deviations eventually give way to large ones. After a few weeks of altering your schedule, you may quickly find you are significantly behind in your studies. The sense of being behind on your schedule will only create added stress that you most certainly don't need during this critical time of your life.

At the end of the day, just remember there is a beautiful simplicity to the bar exam – if you spend the time studying, your odds of passing rise exponentially. Most major bar exam companies will offer some sort of refund if you complete a certain percentage of their program (usually 75%) and do not pass. The reason they can do this is that they know from years of collecting data that people who spend the time studying will pass. So, whenever you are grinding away at practice questions or are bored stiff watching a lecture, pause and mentally note that every second and every minute you are actively engaged in your studies push the meter ever so slightly towards a passing score on the bar exam.

2. Choose the right bar preparation program

In addition to commitment and time, you will need quality study materials to pass the bar exam. If you've fully committed yourself and have allocated all the time in the world to studying, you still won't get very far if you don't have the right materials. The point of this book isn't to talk about the bar prep companies in great detail. There are several of them out there, and they each have their pros and cons. I encourage you to go online and do your research before you purchase a bar package. There is a wealth of information in various forums and articles online that compare the programs, discuss discounts, and offer general information. Make an informed decision.

The big three bar prep companies are Barbri, Themis, and Kaplan. There are others out there, but those three are considered the pillars of bar preparation. For my first bar exam (New York), I used Barbri. I had always been led to believe throughout law school that Barbri was the gold-standard and did not want to take any chances with the first exam. Overall, I was satisfied with Barbri. The user interface was comprehensive and intuitive, the video lectures were well-done (aside from the occasionally obnoxious professor), and the books I received were solid. Overall, I felt like their materials prepared me well for the bar exam.

For my second bar exam (Virginia), I used Themis. I picked Themis the second time for two reasons. First, they were significantly cheaper than Barbri. Second, I did not want to sit through the same set of lecturers I had just watched on the New York bar exam. I had always thought of Themis as the red-headed stepchild to Barbri, but I was pleasantly surprised by the experience. To be honest, if I had to do it all over again, I would pick Themis every time. The interface was more simplistic than Barbri but was nonetheless user friendly and sufficiently comprehensive. While Themis lacks some of the reports and measurement tools of Barbri, you will find they provide more than enough to track your progress. The lecturers and books were on-par with Barbri, and I noticed no substantial difference. The main difference with Themis is that their video lectures are broken down into 10-20 minute segments to keep your attention span. Between those segments, you have quizzes to ensure you are learning. In contrast, some of the Barbri lectures may go on for 3-4 hours without any quizzes to test your learning. Personally, I found the shorter lectures helped to keep my attention as I knew that a break was coming before too long.

One of the main reasons I liked Themis was that they allow you to email substantive law questions to attorneys who will answer them. I literally emailed questions on substantive law over 100 times during my studying and received quick, pleasant, and helpful responses every time. In addition, my assigned essay grader was top notch. She was pleasant, encouraging, and sought to form a bond, unlike the carousel of graders I experienced with Barbri. My advice is that you should do your own research but don't discount Themis just because they're not Barbri. I really enjoyed my Themis experience and would highly recommend them.

For my third bar exam (South Dakota), I did not purchase a bar preparation program but rather acquired a potpourri of books from E-Bay and made a spreadsheet to keep track of my studies. I had a mix of Kaplan, Themis, and Barbri books to study for this exam. The MEE books I had for this bar exam were my only exposure to Kaplan, but I will say the books were more than sufficient, and I saw no difference in quality between these materials and anything produced by Barbri or Themis.

Whatever you do, get the right bar prep materials and don't half-ass it. There is no shortage of information available online to facilitate your research into what will work best for you. Take some time to read review sites and watch videos on YouTube. If you have not taken the MPRE, you can even use some of these programs for that test and get a feel for how well you like the interfaces and content. Invest some time before you decide on a bar preparation program and make an informed choice based on your circumstances. Your existence for the next 10-12 weeks will be largely managed and defined by your bar preparation program, so it is worth the time to make a wise choice.

3. Prepare your physical study space

In addition to bar preparation materials, you will need to prepare the physical space where you will study. You should spend time reflecting in advance on what type of space will work best for you. Some people may decide that working from the comfort of their home is best, and others may decide that working out of their school library is best. Some may decide on an entirely different arrangement altogether. Then some may not have a choice in the matter based on location and logistics. Either way, give some serious thought to where you plan to study and be honest with yourself about which type of space will best enable you to succeed.

On my first bar exam, I initially thought I would go to the library of my local law school to study. My own law school was hundreds of miles away, but I felt that being in the law school environment would help me focus. I quickly found that the hassle of packing up materials and driving to a library every day wasn't worth it. In the end, I studied for all 3 bar exams from the comfort of my home and would do the same again if I took a 4th bar exam.

I was fortunate enough to find a very large, wide desk and a comfortable office chair on the NextDoor app for cheap. These formed the core of my home base for bar studies. Having a large, wide desk was critical, as it allowed me plenty of space for my abundant materials and left room to write and outline when I needed to do so. I stacked all my books in one corner, loaded up on a supply of pens, a notebook, connected my laptop, and created an "office" in the corner of my living room to study for the bar. One thing that I felt helped me was, whichever bar I was studying for, I ensured my desk faced a window, so I could look out into the front yard, sidewalk, and street. Just having the light shining in and occasionally seeing people and vehicles pass kept me feeling connected to society and occasionally provided a needed distraction. Some days, a little wren would perch on the bush just outside the window, only a few feet in front of me. The little bird had no inkling that I was just feet away, and I would pause and watch him groom himself or dig into the bushes. Minor distractions of that nature were welcomed and placing my desk next to a window allowed for these opportunities.

If you study from home, one thing I might suggest is consider getting a tablet to accompany your laptop. I used my laptop for taking notes and quizzes, but whenever I was watching a video lecture, I played the lecture on a tablet next to the computer. The benefit of having a separate tablet to watch lectures from was that I had full access to my computer and did not have to share the screen with a lecturer or toggle between the lecture and my notes. Also, as strange as it may sound, having the lecturer on a separate tablet almost made it seem like there was another person there with me as they had their own designated and exclusive communication device and never intruded on the sanctity of my laptop. If you're thinking you can't afford to spend money on a tablet after you pay a couple thousand dollars for a bar preparation program, rest assured that I found the tablet used on Amazon for less $80.00. It is old and outdated, but it played video lectures just fine and was worth every penny for the benefits it provided during bar study.

4. Incorporate healthy living into your bar study process

Because of the all-consuming nature of bar study, it can be surprisingly easy for your health to go by the wayside. Sitting at a computer for 40-60 hours a week studying to the point of exhaustion is an easy route to gaining weight and getting sick. You should acknowledge this before you begin your studies and plan activities into your bar study process to counter these risks.

As I mentioned, I always made sure to incorporate a mid-day trip to the gym each day. There's nothing that breaks up the monotony and sedentary nature of bar study like riding an elliptical, jogging, or lifting weights. Doing so will not only keep your muscles from atrophy, but the exercise will give you a much-needed boost of energy to help you jump right back in to the second half of your study day.

As an animal advocate, I would be remiss not to mention that those with pets should make sure to incorporate their needs into your plans. If you have a dog or perhaps multiple dogs, they're going to get bored sitting around watching you on the computer. Make walking them a regular part of your routine. You'll get some fresh air, clear your head, and your dog(s) will appreciate you for it. If you have a cat, a gerbil, a parakeet, or any other living creature, make sure you are carving out the appropriate time in your day to give them the attention they deserve.

Bar study is also an unfortunately opportune time to overeat and gain wait. There are few pleasantries during bar study, and a handful of chips or some candy can often be an easy outlet for your anxiety and boredom. During my New York and South Dakota bar studies, I probably put on 10 pounds just from absentminded snacking as a way to try to fill the tedium. During my Virginia bar studies, I was more conscious of this risk and made an effort to incorporate regular glasses of water and healthy snacks. Water is almost never a bad thing. Try to set a goal to drink a glass of water after every hour or two of studying. The water will fill you up, eliminate cravings, and you'll be able to study a lot more effectively knowing you're taking measures to avoid gaining weight along the way.

Another thing to keep in mind is the toll that bar study will take on your back. Hour after hour hunched over the computer is not good for your spinal column. Consider going online or to your local fitness store and purchasing a foam roller. I went on Amazon and purchased a "lower back stretcher" from a company called Spinal Labs and consider it one of the best bar study purchases I made. At the end of a hard day of bar study, I would lie on the stretcher for a few minutes and release some of the accumulated tension from my lower back. This small ritual became one of a handful of tiny rewards that I came to look forward to at the end of each day. Bar study is like that. Sometimes, you have to keep yourself going with the little things. Find a way to take care of your back and you'll be better off for it in the long run.

Last, as with any activity that is both mentally and physically exhausting, be aware that it is incredibly easy to get sick during bar studies. Studying for the bar exam is painful enough, but doing so while your nose is stuffed and you're coughing every 30 seconds is untenable. Ironically, on all three of my bar exams, I avoided getting a cold, but the day before the New York bar exam, I came down with a severe cold. I can tell you from experience that taking a bar exam while worrying about sniffling and coughing provides a host of mental distractions that are completely unwelcome. At the end of the day, everyone has their own routine for staying healthy. Mine includes heavy doses of zinc and Airborne at the first sign of a sickness. Whatever your routine is, be vigilant and proactive in avoiding sickness during bar studies.

5. Complete the Character and Fitness application early

While the actual bar exam will take most of your focus, the exam isn't the only milestone you need to achieve to practice law in your desired jurisdiction. The character and fitness application can be a daunting activity in its own right, but if you do not complete it or do not pass it, it means nothing that you have passed the bar exam.

Strive to complete your character and fitness application as early as possible, ideally before the bar exam. Some states require the application before the bar exam, and others do not allow it until after the exam. As with everything, be sure to check your jurisdiction's bar examiner website for details.

Put plainly, you do not want to be messing with your character and fitness application while you are supposed to be focused on studying. It is a needless and unwelcome distraction. Finish the character and fitness application as soon as possible. If your jurisdiction does not allow you to submit it until after the exam, that does not prevent you from gathering all the information you will need in advance. If you can submit before the exam, do so by all means.

These applications vary by state, and I have seen a wide range of requests and formalities across the three states where I have taken the bar. I have been asked for reference letters, addresses for the past 10 years, employment verification forms, contact information for prior employers, personal references, police reports, fingerprint cards (state police and FBI), credit reports, and all manner of other things. I estimate, for each of the applications I have completed, I spent between 15 and 30 hours collecting and gathering information. The process of collecting this information and completing the application is tedious and dry. As with the bar exam, there is no way around it, unfortunately.

Be aware that the character and fitness application is not self-contained. What I mean by this is that it is not something where you can sit down in front of the computer and bang it out in a day. You will need to plan ahead. Other people will need to write you letters, you will be asked for information you may need to request from government agencies, you will have to find a notary to notarize (several) forms for you.

My best advice is to dive into the character and fitness application as soon as humanly possible. Read the forms and make yourself a checklist of what is needed. Then sequence how you will get that information. Some of it, you will need to request, and it will take weeks, and some you can just type up immediately on your computer. Set a target date to complete it, make a plan, and get it done. You absolutely do not want to deal with this while you are studying.

Once your application is submitted, different jurisdictions have different protocol as far as how they screen your applications. In New York, I had a face-to-face interview with an examiner before I was sworn in. In Virginia and South Dakota, I know the paperwork was thoroughly vetted, as references told me they were being contacted, but I never had to do a face-to-face interview. Read the materials for your specific jurisdiction carefully and be prepared. Although this may seem like an ancillary task that is not central to the bar exam, you should take it seriously and plan early to get it done.

6. Find comfort on the Internet (if it suits you)

During the course of my studies, I found it helpful to have some outlet to connect with the outside world. I was away from school for all three bar exams I studied for, so I was not around former classmates. If you're the type of person who wants to "stay connected," then you may find some value in online forums.

The one I found most useful was the Top Law Bar Exam Forum (http://www.top-law-schools.com/forums). Here, you can find all manner of posts from people selling materials, discussing study habits, talking about Barbri/Themis lecturers, discussing logistics of the test site, etc. I found that watching this forum during bar study was a helpful vehicle to stay connected to the outside world and calibrate my performance with others. Occasionally, someone will start a thread on a specific state, and then you can find kinship with fellow students prepping for your exam. During mock exam times for the big bar prep companies, people will often post their scores, so you can get a sense of how you're doing against others (in addition to the scores you get through your respective bar preparation program).

Another helpful resource is Reddit. While more irreverent at times, Reddit usually has several threads and sub-threads about bar exam preparation. You can often find some useful commentary or information here to stay connected with the outside world and get an anecdotal sense of how you're progressing against others.

Obviously, take everything you read with a grain of salt on either of these sites. The sample sizes are small and random, and you never know whether someone is being entirely truthful. That said, I found these online forums to be a somewhat useful tool for getting a casual pulse check on my progress.

CONCLUSION

In the end, your preparation for the bar exam may be just as critical as your actual study time. By setting the stage for a successful study process, you will free your mind from unnecessary stressors and anxieties and significantly ease your suffering along the journey to (hopefully) passing the bar exam.

1. Fully commit yourself to bar study; don't half-ass it.
2. Clear your calendar and treat bar study as a full time job for the next 10-12 weeks.
3. Carefully research your bar study program and choose one that best meets your circumstances.
4. Trust in the primary bar preparation companies – they are tried and proven.
5. Create a physical study space where you will be engaged and comfortable.
6. Incorporate healthy habits into your study plan – exercise, eat right, drink water, get plenty of sleep, and don't forget to take care of your animals.

7. Knock out your character and fitness application as early as possible, so you don't have to worry about it while you are studying.
8. If it suits you, stay connected to Internet forums to get an occasional pulse check on your progress relative to the outside world.

CHAPTER 3

Multistate Performance Test (MPT)

1. Overview

As of this writing, over 30 states have adopted the Uniform Bar Exam (UBE), which includes the Multistate Performance Test (MPT). Several other states that do not officially use the UBE include the MPT as a component of their testing. Consequently, the vast majority of states will include at least one MPT question, and most people reading this will need to hone these skills in order to succeed.

Depending on your jurisdiction, you will need to complete either one or two MPT problems. Each problem is 90 minutes in length. The MPT is intended to test your abilities to function like an actual attorney under timed conditions. Unlike the other sections of the bar exam, the MPT is not intended to test your recollection of black letter law. Everything you need to succeed in the MPT is given to you, and you do not need to know or memorize anything.

In essence, the MPT simulates a senior attorney giving you an assignment to draft some type of legal document that you must complete in 90 minutes. You will be given a packet of materials including two distinct sections: (1) the File and (2) the Library. Most importantly, the File contains a memo with instructions on your overall assignment. In addition, the File includes all other relevant **facts** of the particular case. In contrast, the Library contains all of the **law**, which may take the form of statutes, case law, administrative code, etc. Each MPT is different, and your assignments will differ. Some ask you to draft an objective letter, while others may ask for a persuasive brief, a piece of legislation, a demand letter, or even a contract.

2. Master the MPT to gain points

Because the MPT is a closed-universe problem and you do not need to memorize anything, many people will give short shrift to this portion of the test and spend less time here. That is a grave mistake.

The MPT is a prime opportunity to make up points that you will surely lose elsewhere in the exam. Nailing the MPT will help cover deficiencies in other areas of your performance and create some flexibility for you should you perform below expectations on other areas of the exam. Be aware, however, that some states will combine your score between Day One and Day Two to meet a minimum threshold, and some require you to meet a threshold for each day. What this means is that, in some cases, extra points on your MPT can help offset deficiencies on both your MEE and your MBE, whereas in other states, it will only offset deficiencies on your MEE. Either way, a positive MPT score will help you in the long run.

Overall, do not dismiss the MPT as something you should focus less on. Focus on being that person who masters the MPT and is ready for any type of problem you may get. I guarantee those points will come in handy on your overall bar score. As you go through bar study and hear friends talk about how miserable and tedious the MPT is, strive to be the contrarian who finds delight in the MPT because you recognize the importance of mastering these skills in the overall scheme of the bar exam.

3. Practice, practice, practice

So, how do you master the MPT, especially when the type of document you may be writing can change with every problem? The simple answer is that you practice repeatedly and build the core skills that will be used, no matter what type of problem you face. Regardless of whether you are asked to draft a brief, a piece of legislation, a letter, or even a judicial opinion, there are certain fundamental skills you can hone that will serve you well on test day.

I recommend doing **no less** than 6 practice MPT's during the course of your bar preparation. For each of my bar exams, I did between 6 and 9 full practice MPTs. That may seem like a lot, considering each is 90 minutes, but when test day came, I was always thankful to have done so many practice problems. By doing a lot of practice problems, you build a set of core skills and techniques that are easily transferrable to the real exam.

First, you build the mental and physical stamina needed to complete these problems. I cannot overstate this enough. The MPT is unlike the MBE and the MEE. On the MBE, the questions come in rapid fire, and you are ideally spending less than 2 minutes working with the set of facts and issues. Even on the MEE, the problems only last 30 minutes and may be no more than 4-6 paragraphs in length. The MPT is different. You will be faced with anywhere from 10 to 18 pages worth of material that you need to read, process, digest, and work with in a span of 90 minutes. Reading all that information and constantly sifting through it as you write your answer can be exhausting. By doing multiple MPT problems, you teach your brain and your body what that exercise will be like and you become accustomed to the rigors needed to grind through these problems.

If test day is the first time you sit down and work through a 90 minute problem, you are in serious trouble. Not only are you ill-prepared for the MPT problems, but since most jurisdictions seem to conduct the MPT in the morning of Day One, you are setting yourself up for a long afternoon of MEE problems if you leave the morning feeling exhausted and frustrated. Don't do that. Take a minute to think about how you would like to feel after the morning session of Day One – confident, invigorated, and optimistic. In order to feel that way, you need to prepare for the MPT problems and make sure you nail these problems.

Furthermore, if your exam consists of 2 MPT problems, at least once during your test preparation, you should do back to back MPT problems under timed conditions, so you get a sense for what test day will be like. MPT problems are mentally exhausting, but you will need to condition yourself to be able to complete one problem and immediately shift to another without a break.

Overall, your goal is to make sure you practice enough problems beforehand, so you become accustomed to the feel of working through an MPT problem (or two). Building that muscle and mental memory will be invaluable on test day.

Second, by doing practice problems, you

will get a sense of the timing, which is critical. Even though your practice problems may entail creating different types of documents than you experience on test day, the length and the depth of the material will be comparable. You will tune your brain and your body to be able to read through the material quickly enough to finish on time. You will start to hardwire your body to feel when you should stop reading and start outlining. Practice will help calibrate your internal clock to the examiner's expectations.

Third, working through practice MPT problems will allow you to develop and refine your particular process or approach to outlining and answering the problems. With every MPT problem, you will have a File and a Library. In your File, you will have a memo that provides you with your task. As you work through problems, you will start to develop a process whereby you mark facts and issues and you designate them to specific parts of your outline (see below for more details). These practice problems are the time to develop your personal process. Exam day is not the time to figure out your methods for solving a problem.

Finally, doing practice problems will sharpen your reading comprehension and analysis skills. By timing yourself through numerous practice MPT's, you are practicing your ability to read dense material quickly, to spot issues, and to mentally correlate disparate pieces of information. These are skills you will need on test day, and doing at least 6 MPT practice problems before the exam will help you refine these skills along the way.

4. Approach to the MPT

Regardless of the type of document you are asked to create on test day, you should be able to define your own approach to handling MPT problems. By "approach," I simply mean the methodology by which you will read a problem, create your outline, and write your answer. In this section, I will describe my approach, but you should be thoughtful about what works best for you. Bar preparation is the time to refine this approach and fine tune it, so you can unleash it on test day.

a) Read the name of the problem while you're waiting to begin

Before the clock even starts, you will be handed a booklet and told not to open it. On the cover of the booklet is the name of your problem. This is information. Don't sit there and stare at the clock or chew on your pencil. Use every second to your advantage and do not waste this time.

As you are sitting there waiting for the proctor to announce that you may begin, make a conscious effort to see what you can glean from the cover of your problem. This is not an exact science, but you can get a jumpstart on the problem.

Below are some made-up examples and things you may learn from them:

State v. Edwards – The fact that State appears in the title may give you a clue that this problem relates to a criminal matter.

Franklin v. Sunny Day Elder Care – You know from your practice problems that "Franklin" is the name of the fictitious jurisdiction used in MPT problems, so you know now that the government is involved in this case. "Sunny Day Elder Care" tells you that a caretaking business is involved. This could suggest the problem is related to the violation of some municipal or administrative ordinance. It also tells you that your facts are likely to be dealing with things like medical care, therapy, older people, etc.

Jenkins v. ABC Automotive – This sounds like a civil case, potentially a suit involving a faulty automobile repair or some torts liability. You have what appears to be the name of a private individual ("Jenkins") against an automotive repair business.

Of course, you will never truly know what the problem is about until you dive in, but when you are faced with free information and the clock isn't running, you should not waste the opportunity. Even if it saves you 5 seconds of time to get your head wrapped around the type of problem, that could mean a point or two in the long run. Every point counts, and consequently, every second does as well.

b) Scan and digest the Table of Contents

Once the proctor announces the clock has started, you will unseal your MPT. When you open your MPT, you will see a Table of Contents. Do not skip this. This is a one page document that lays out all the materials before you. I do not recommend spending more than 30 seconds on it, but stop and read through it and make an effort to see what you can learn.

The table of contents will list the File first, with all the documents included, and then the Library. Quickly scan each line and see what you're dealing with. Almost always, the first document in the File will be a memo, which is your set of directions. Look through the rest and see what you have – do you have transcripts, interview notes, investigations reports? Some materials are easier to process than others. For instance, deposition and interview notes tend to be quick reads with significant conversational fluff, whereas other things, like a magazine article or a contract, may require more of your time.

Look next to the Library and see what you're working with. How many cases are there? Cases tend to take the longest time to read and are usually 2-3 pages in length. If I look and see only 1 case, that is usually good news. The rest will likely be statutes or administrative codes. If I look and see 3 cases, I use that information to prepare myself mentally for some intensive reading.

In general, take a few seconds before you dive in to skim the table of contents and glean what you can. What you are doing is building a mental foundation of what this problem is all about and starting to put the pieces together. At this point, after having read the title of the MPT and the table of contents, you should generally know: (1) what the case is about at a very high level and (2) where you expect to spend the majority of your time.

c) Read the memo and write your task statement

The memo is the single most important document in your MPT packet. The memo includes your instructions for this task. There is no mistake that will be more damaging than to misunderstand or not follow the instructions in the memo.

The memo will tell you who is assigning your task (usually a senior attorney), what the context of the issue is, and what you are being asked to do. The memo will basically include your requirements for completing this assignment. It will tell you what type of document to create, what to include, and what not to include.

If you create the wrong document, include the wrong information, structure your document incorrectly, or include sections you did not need to spend time on, you have shot yourself in the foot and wasted easy points. You have also planted a data point with your grader that you are careless. That is not the impression you want someone to have as they begin grading a very large portion of your overall exam grade. Whatever you do, take the time to read the memo at least twice.

As you read the memo, your most important takeaway is to understand what, specifically, is being asked of you. Once you have read the memo and fully understand, you should type out a quick synopsis of what your task is on your computer in the exam software. Simply write "TASK" followed by a bulleted list of what you are being asked to do and include anything you should not focus on. Your goal here is to create a 2-3 line summary in your writing of what you are being asked to do. Once you have written that, read the memo once more and compare it to your task statement and make sure they are aligned.

By forcing yourself to type out your task statement, first, you are embedding in your head what your assignment is. The physical act of typing out this statement makes you process it through your brain. Second, the physical act of comparing what you wrote with what is in the memo serves as a safety check to ensure you are on the right path.

Note that this task statement SHOULD BE DELETED once you have finished typing your whole answer. This statement serves only as your roadmap and is not a part of your answer. (If it is easier for you to handwrite your task statement on the exam booklet, then go that route; personally, I find typing it saves time and makes for easier reference.)

Once you have completed your full MPT answer and before you submit, go back once more and read your task statement, compare it with the memo to ensure you have addressed all key points, then delete it.

d) Create a skeleton outline

In most cases, after you have read the memo, you will have enough information to create a skeleton outline for your answer. For example, the memo may say: "I want you to write a persuasive brief analyzing the elements of negligence and applying the facts of Ms. Jones' slip and fall at the grocery store. Do not include a statement of facts and do not discuss causation." That type of memo gives you a clear understanding of what your answer will look like. You can then type out an outline and include sections for Element 1, Element 2, Element 3, and Element 4.

Although some memos will not give you something as tangible as the negligence example above, they will still usually give you enough to create a very rough outline even if you have to amend it later. The gist of this part of the approach is to create some sort of framework based on the information you have from the memo.

Note that, even though a problem may ask you to analyze something you already know (such as the elements of negligence), you should not always assume that what you know from law school matches what you will read in the Library of your MPT. While negligence is fairly straightforward, there is the possibility that the state of Franklin may include a separate element or may break one element into two elements, etc. The point is, stay away from injecting outside information into the MPT problem. The MPT is intended to be a self-contained universe, and you should not include extrinsic information.

Overall, after reading the memo, you should have a rough idea of what your outline will look like. Take the time and type out those headers on your computer. You will be amazed at how the simple task of having headers will make you feel mentally. You're now starting to build your answer versus flailing around on a blank screen. Even though you have literally typed a handful of headers, psychologically, you have started your answer at just a few minutes into the exam, and that can be mentally empowering.

e) Read the Library and start populating your outline as you read

Now you understand what you're being asked to do, and you should have a rough skeleton outline. Many people would continue sequentially and dive into the rest of the File, but you shouldn't. By reading the facts in the File without understanding the applicable law, you are wasting time. In legal practice, the facts are applied to the law, not the other way around. You want to understand your baseline legal rules before processing the facts. In addition, the facts are much easier to remember than the law. You want to spend your early time (when there is still a lot of it and your brain is fresh) processing the core law that will come into play with your problem.

After you have read the memo and completed your task statement, flip immediately to the Library and read it entirely. You are likely to have a mixture of statutes, administrative codes, and case law.

Depending on the type of problem you have, you may be able to add to your outline as you are reading the statutes. For example, if your memo asked you to analyze the facts of the case according to the elements of the Franklin common law crime of burglary, and the first page of your Library is the Franklin statute that lays out the elements of burglary, you can start typing these into your outline as headers.

Similarly, if you read a passage in a statute or case that you absolutely know you will use, type it then and there. For instance, say your problem is about common carrier liability and you come across a case that says, "In State v. Jones, the court observed that the concept of common carrier liability stems from the premise that those who take responsibility for passengers are bound to ensure their safety." That should immediately stick out to you as a passage that you will want to use. The Library is giving you contextual information directly related to what you are analyzing. You should read that and immediately think, "This is a good introductory line to my analysis." Type it now while you're looking at it. You know you will use it, so don't waste your time having to find it later. Type out the part you will use in the section of your outline that seems most relevant.

As much as you can, you should try to do this. Look for passages of cases or statutes that you are absolutely certain will be used in your answer. Grab them now and type them into the respective spot on your outline. That way, once you have finished reading the Library and before you have even cracked open the bulk of the File, you already have a ton of written information in your outline that is easy to work with by adding introductory language, copying and pasting, etc.

By typing information you know you will use as you come across it in your reading, you are building your answer as you read versus reading everything and trying to remember where it was later when you need it. Your outline won't look pretty and will require a ton of work to polish it and connect the pieces, but you are effectively laying down the concrete blocks of your foundation while you read. Once you've done that, you'll go back and layer in your facts and a coat of polish, and you will have a solid answer. I think most people read everything before they begin writing, but if you write while you read, you're making best use of your time and avoiding having to search for information later and read things a second or third time.

However, sometimes it may not be obvious that you will use information as you read it. What should you do? If you see a passage you think may be useful, but you're just not sure, do not type it at this point. You could end up wasting time typing something that is not relevant. Instead, mark them in a fashion that makes sense to you. One thing I would do is designate parts of my outline and make corresponding marks. For instance, if I had an outline that was the four elements of negligence, and I later read a part of a case that dealt with duty, I would mark it with a "D". If I saw something on causation, I would mark it with a "C" and damages perhaps a "DAM". That way, as I work through filling in my outline, I can quickly skim back through the cases looking for the respective codes and easily pull out that information without having to hunt for it.

There are a couple of other key points to mention. First, you should realize that not every word in the Library is useful to your case, and if you try to fit everything into your answer, you will run out of time and lose points. Just remember as you read that not everything is meaningful, so do not feel obligated to type everything into your outline or even mark it as something for possible use later. Some things are included to test your ability to identify trivial content. Be aware of that.

Second, you should remember it is critical to include citations for anything you pull from the Library. The examiners want to know where you got information, so as you are writing it into your outline, include a basic citation to signal the source of the information. This can be as simple as the case name or the section of the statute. Now is not the time to practice Blue Book skills. Simply write enough to let the grader know where you sourced the information and move on.

By the time you have finished reading

your Library (and before you have even read the File beyond the memo), you should have: (1) an outline, (2) key passages of law written into the relevant sections of your outline, and (3) other passages of law marked according to which portion of the outline they relate to if you decide later you need to use them. At this point, you should be about 25-30 minutes into your 90 minutes. You've got at least an hour to go, and you probably already have 30% of your answer written. Your fellow test takers may well have written nothing and are still reading through the File with a blank computer screen staring them in the face. You're ahead of the game. Keep moving.

f) Read the File and keep populating your outline as you read

Now comes the easy part. You've processed and digested everything in the Library; facts are so much easier to remember than law. Flip back to the File and read from the first document past the memo.

You're likely to find a wide assortment of information here. It seems that most Files contain some type of interview or deposition transcript. These are easy. About 30% of these will contain worthless information, such as pleasantries between the attorney and the interviewee or other such information that fills the void in day to day conversations between people. Do not assume that something is worthless, though, as it could contain a key fact, but be prepared to scan quickly past any useless fluff.

In addition to deposition or interview transcripts, you might find a range of documents, including advertisements, letters, receipts, notes, contracts, or memorandums. Read through this information carefully. Follow the same exact process you did with the Library – either type things into your outline if you know you will use them or mark them with the designated section of where they will go if you end up using them. If there's something you're just not sure about, mark it with a question mark or something else to let yourself know it may have value, so you can find it later.

g) Pause and take stock of your situation

Once you have finished reading the Library and the File, stop and take a conscious pause. Your mind will likely be flooded with information and racing to piece it together. It will behoove you to stop and let it all settle for a moment. Flip back to the memo and read your task again. Then think back to everything you have read and make absolute certain your outline is appropriate based on what is being asked of you. Does your outline cover the key elements? Does it adequately represent the law you just read? Does it address the requirements of the memo? If it does, great, you can move on. If it does not, now is the time to modify your outline before you begin writing in earnest. The outline is the framework for your entire answer. If your outline is constructed poorly and not how the examiner would expect to see it, you will lose points, even if you cover most of the key points somewhere in your answer. By poorly constructing the framework of your answer, you are making the examiner work to find information, and there is no guarantee they will find it. You want your outline to be in the exact structure and format they expect. The best way to do that is to pause, reflect on the memo, reflect on the law, and make sure that what you are about to start writing is formatted in the way they expect. Once you are confident your outline is formatted appropriately, get to writing.

h) Write your answer

By this point, what you are doing is filling in the blanks of your outline, ideally with facts, as you should have the passages of law written and grouped accordingly. Start through each section of your outline sequentially and start writing it out. Follow the formatting instructions you have been given. In most cases, you will be writing the law (which you already have) and then applying it to the facts. Go through your statements of law and polish them. Place introductory clauses, fix the punctuation, and merge statements into a cohesive fashion, so it reads like a clear legal document. Then apply the facts. The law should be crystal clear to you at this point, and the facts are easy to remember, so this should largely be an exercise in writing.

i) Review and polish your answer

At this point, you should have anywhere from 10-20 minutes remaining. Now is the time to read, refine, and polish your answer. Start from the top and make sure you read the task statement you wrote one last time. This is your final safety check. Think about whether you truly addressed the task you were assigned. If you did, delete the task statement. If you did not, fix what you missed. Once you have done that, read through your answer from top to bottom. Make sure it is clear, the grammar and punctuation are proper, your quotations are correct, and your citations are accurate. If you have time, you can even underline or italicize case names for extra cleanliness. Check your headers and ensure they make sense. Basically, proofread your answer and pretend you are an examiner who just opened it. See if it reads well and is clearly written. Use this remaining time to fix any issues.

If you complete this final polish and

have time remaining, you can do one of two things. If your jurisdiction does 2 MPTs back to back, you can begin the next one. Otherwise, you should re-read the memo one last time and make certain you have not missed anything. Then scan back through the File and see if you marked any important facts you wanted to mention and did not. If you see any you missed, quickly add them. If you covered all the key facts, take one last pass through the Library and make sure you understood and addressed the key points of law. Once all this is done, you have done what you need to do to succeed on the MPT.

CONCLUSION

The MPT often gets overshadowed by the MBE and the MEE as the red-headed stepchild of the bar exam. MPT points are just as meaningful to your final score as any other section. Consciously decide you will master the MPT and dedicate the time and effort it deserves.

1. Practice, practice, practice; do no less than 6 practice MPT problems during your studies.
2. If your jurisdiction entails 2 MPTs, do at least one round of practice where you do back to back MPTs under timed conditions.
3. Develop and practice your approach to the MPT:
   a. Glean whatever you can from the problem title and Table of Contents.

   b. Read the memo and ensure you are crystal clear on what your task is.

c. Write out your task statement and compare it to the memo.

d. Draft a skeleton outline.

e. Read the Library and add key passages of law to your outline or mark them for reference later.

f. Read the File and add key facts to your outline or mark them for reference later.

g. Type out your answer by filling in the gaps in your outline.

h. h. Review and polish your answer.

CHAPTER 4

Multistate Essay Examination (MEE)

1. Overview

In addition to those states that administer the UBE, several other states include the Multistate Essay Examination (MEE) as part of their exams. In addition, the vast majority of states not administering the MEE also require some form of essay. Thus, the materials in this section should be broadly relevant to most bar exams. However, as with everything about the bar exam, be certain you understand the requirements and format of your state's examination before you begin your studies and craft your approach accordingly.

The MEE typically entails a series of timed essay questions. Students will generally complete 6 essay questions in a span of 3 hours, allowing for 30 minutes per question. These questions are to be completed in one sitting, and students are free to allocate as much time to each question as they deem appropriate, although the total time allowed will not exceed three hours.

MEE questions are intended to test issue spotting, understanding fundamental legal principles, and the ability to analyze and apply facts to the law in a timed situation. Unlike the MPT, MEE questions move more rapidly. Your fact patterns are typically 4-8 paragraphs in length, and with each MEE question, you will be asked a series of sub-questions about the fact pattern, usually between 2 and 4.

2. Practice, practice, practice

It should come as no surprise that the key factor

for success on the MEE portion of your exam is practice. Just like all other areas of this exam, completing practice problems will build your muscle memory, allow you to calibrate your internal clock, and expose you to substantial areas of the law in real-life situations versus simply as black letter law on a page without real application.

You should make it your goal to complete no less than 60 MEE practice problems during the course of your studies. The more problems you complete, the better off you will be. During my New York exam, I completed approximately 65 through Barbri. During Virginia, I completed around 110 as Themis required many more essay problems. For South Dakota, I completed 84 practice problems. My personal opinion is that you are doing yourself a grave disservice by completing less than 60 MEE practice problems, and even that number should be the bare minimum. I have spoken to people who have completed anywhere from 5-15 practice problems and can't help but think they are setting themselves up for failure.

In completing your practice MEE problems, there are two things to keep in mind. First, you do not need to write out each and every problem. The key objective in completing MEE practice problems is spotting issues and recognizing and applying the appropriate law. While writing full answers also helps practice your timing and ability to string together sentences and analysis, you will be able to cover a wider scope of potential issues you might encounter on the exam if you fully write about half and outline the other half of your practice problems.

Second, as you are taking MEE practice problems, be sure to do more than one at a time. While it is fine to complete one at a time as you get started, eventually, you should be stringing together, 2, 3, and finally 6 problems in a row in timed sessions to get your mind and body acclimated to being able to shift between problems and keep your momentum moving. You should complete at least one round of 6 practice questions under timed conditions before you take the real exam.

The MEE represents a substantial portion of your exam. As such, success is critical. The best way to prepare yourself for success is to train your mind repeatedly in realistic, simulations of what the exam will be like. The exam is not about reading black letter law from a book and remembering rules. The exam is about looking at a fact pattern, understanding the issues, then applying that black letter law to the facts. On the MEE, you only get that through doing practice problems.

Do as many MEE practice problems as possible and rest assured that, by the time test day comes, you will be well-prepared to face the MEE portion of the exam. You want test day to be about processing a different set of facts. Everything else should be finely tuned by that point. You will know how to structure your answer, how to manage your time, how to spot issues, and how to analyze legal problems. Building those skills in advance of the exam comes through constant repetition and practice. There is no other way around it.

3. View practice problems as "learning," not just "practice"

One mistake that many seem to make is they believe the only way they are truly learning is by reading outlines and watching videos. Inversely, they believe doing practice questions simply tests that learning and is not actually the process of learning. Do not look at practice problems in that light. Practice problems are your opportunity to test what you learn, but you should also view practice problems as a learning experience in their own right. In fact, I would argue that learning by reading the answers on a practice problem is more effective than actually reading through straight outlines.

When you complete a practice problem or problems, methodically review the answer to the problem. The major bar prep companies provide comprehensive answers to all practice problems. In particular, I find Barbri's answer checklist very helpful in gauging success on practice problems, as it provides a binary means to measure your performance.

Carefully read through the answers to the question and assess your performance thoughtfully and realistically. It does you no good to fool yourself and avoid recognizing missed points on the answer. While you may temporarily feel better, when exam day comes, you will be less prepared. Now is not the time to coddle your ego. Take a stark and harsh look at your performance. As you read through the answers, you should do two things.

First, validate the portions you got right.

Did you get all the rules right? Are they worded correctly? Did you properly apply the facts to the law? Did you miss some important facts?

Second, study the portions you got wrong. This is where the key learning comes and where your knowledge base will grow. Make certain you understand why you missed a particular section. Did you misstate the rule? Did you simply miss an issue? Did you miss an element of the rule? Do you not understand what is being discussed?

You should track and record all the sections you missed. This is what I did. For every rule of law I missed on an essay, I went back into my outline for that specific subject and verified that I indeed had the rule of law written and had simply forgotten it. If I had the rule of law, I would read it silently to myself and process it. Remember, so much of bar exam success is about how many times you can process information through your brain. If I did not have the rule of law, I would type it into my outline. Again, the physical act of typing something processes information through your brain. If I found myself continually missing the same rule, I would highlight it and add emphasis for when I reviewed later. As an example, I distinctly remember that I missed numerous Contracts practice problems because I could not remember the Mailbox Rule did not apply to options contracts and, at the end of the day, after continually going back and reviewing that part of my outline, that section was highlighted in bright colors and the font was made large so I would definitely remember it next time.

Next, after you have reviewed and possibly edited your outline, start a completely separate outline to capture and aggregate all the rules you have missed. You can think of this as your "Outline of Missed Answers" where you dump all the rules you have missed along the way. You can use this same outline for both the MEE and MBE, or you can make one for each. I would recommend making just one for both, as the rules are the rules regardless of which portion of the exam they apply. Every time you miss a rule of law, go type it on your "Outline of Missed Answers." My outline was grouped by subject area, so every time I missed a Torts rule, I added it to that section. Every time I missed a Criminal Law rule, I added it to that section. At the end of the day, it is just one outline that aggregates all the rules of law you missed.

You may think this is repetitive and a waste

of time, but I assure you it is not. Once again, by forcing yourself to physically type out the rule of law a second time (in addition to your main outline), you are forcing your brain to process the information once more. The fact that you are adding it to the "Outline of Missed Answers" will also send a subtle cue to your brain that this is a problem area that you need to be aware of, thus further emphasizing the need to remember the information. In addition, your "Outline of Missed Answers" will grow and become an incredibly useful tool in your studies. Every so often, print a fresh version of the outline and look it over. I found great value in taking this outline to the gym occasionally and reading while I rode an elliptical. This outline is more enjoyable to review than most because it skims through a variety of subjects versus being a monotonous deep-dive into one particular subject.

Use your missed practice answers as a learning experience. Harvest your missed answers for rules of law; force yourself to review those rules by typing them in both your main outline and your new "Outline of Missed Answers."

4. Approach to the MEE

The MEE moves more rapidly than the MPT. In addition, you will be faced with more unique MEE questions, and typically, the MEE counts more than the MPT (but check your jurisdiction). Having a tried and true process to work through MEE questions efficiently and productively is critical. Everyone works in their own manner, so determine what works best for you. Below is the process I followed.

a) Read the call of the question

Your bar prep companies will drive this home, and this is undoubtedly your first step. Before you begin to digest a voluminous fact pattern, skip to the call of the question and read what you are being asked to do. You can glean critical information from the call of the question.

First, you will likely be able to tell what type of question you are facing. If you see "Did the court err in denying the motion to dismiss for lack of subject matter jurisdiction?" you know you are likely dealing with a Civil Procedure question. In contrast, if you see "How will the court distribute the proceeds of John's estate?" you know you are dealing with a Wills question. Being able to get your head around the type of question quickly will help you direct your brain to the area of law you will need to produce.

Second, understanding the call of the question will tell you how many parts of the answer you will need to write. If you see two sub-questions, you know you will likely be doing somewhat in-depth analysis on two legal rules. In contrast, if you see four sub-questions, you know you will be writing shorter answers and likely touching on more areas of law a little more shallowly. This helps you to get your head around the type of answer you will be writing.

b) Quickly jot down rules that are implicated

As you read the calls of the question, legal rules should trigger in your head. A question asking about whether a trust modification is proper should trigger certain rules; a question about whether a trial court's denial of a motion can be appealed immediately should trigger different rules, and a question about the priority of security interests should trigger an entirely different set.

In many cases, you know from the call of the question just what rules are involved in your answer. If you can infer this from the question, jot down those rules immediately. I'm not talking about writing full rule statements, but next to the question, jot down a mnemonic or some words that will help you remember the rule. The benefit is that you are already starting your answer before you have read the facts. You've got a head start on the problem and are just seconds into reading. In addition, you never want your mind to go blank. If you read something and think of the rule but then read the fact pattern, there is always the chance you will forget the rule after processing all the facts. Why take that chance? Jot down the rule immediately as you recognize you will need it.

c) Write your headings

After you have read the call of the question and jotted down any key rules, type your question headings. Yes, I said to start typing before you have even read the fact pattern, and I will explain why.

Let's say you read the call of the question, and it says:

> (a) How should the court rule on Citizen's challenge to City's ordinance prohibiting leafletting on the public sidewalk?

> (b) On what grounds can Citizen challenge his arrest for disrupting the council meeting?

For starters, you know you're probably dealing with Constitutional Law issues. In reading the calls of the question, you should have spotted a First Amendment issue in (a). Sub-question (b) is a little more nebulous but also sounds like a Constitutional Law issue, and the fact that (a) deals with Con Law is probably a good indicator. Either way, you know now that you are likely dealing with a Constitutional Law issue related to free speech under the First Amendment.

Turn now to the blank screen on your laptop and type "(a) How should the court rule on Citizen's challenge to City's ordinance prohibiting leafletting on the public sidewalk?"

Wait, what? You're asking me to type the exact question? Yes, I am. There are several reasons for this. Once again, typing the information processes it through your brain. So, while you have already read the call of the question, being forced to type it drills it into your brain and reinforces what you need to answer to succeed.

Second, in the time it takes you to type this information, your brain is processing it and subconsciously searching for rules of law related to this area. The typing will trigger your brain to begin this search of the memory banks.

Third, by typing this question, you are already starting your answer. You know you will need headings for each of your answers, and every bar prep company will teach you to answer the question asked directly. What better way to make a heading for your answer and make things easy on your grader than to ask the exact same question they want you to answer? An examiner who reviews a problem with a heading that mirrors the question will be able to review and grade the answer more rapidly than one who reads something that may be worded in such a way that it raises questions as to whether the examinee even understood the question being posed. You do not want to create such doubts as a first impression. Work with what is given to you and start your answer with the question posed.

Finally (and this is not intentional), when you read a problem and start typing within seconds, the person next to you is likely to have some sort of reaction. I remember, in South Dakota, when I started typing seconds after getting the problem and the rest of the room was silent, you could almost feel a tangible expression of anxiety from the people around me, wondering, "How does he know the answer already?" Well, I didn't know the answer. I was just typing the header. But the fact that they're wondering what I am doing means they are not focusing on their problems, and their lack of focus gives me an edge in the long run. It is not something you intentionally want to do, but as a byproduct of your approach, it provides a subtle competitive advantage.

d) Carefully read the problem; keep facts straight and identify issues and associated rules

Alright, by this point, you have read the call of the question, determined what type of problem you're dealing with, jotted down any reminders of rule statements you will need, and typed out the headers for your answers. You should be less than 2-3 minutes into your allotted time, and you're well on your way. Now is the time to read through the whole problem.

Obviously, start from the beginning of the problem and read through carefully. As you are reading, it may help you to draw a quick diagram of the different characters or situations. I often find, in certain problem types, a diagram will help. For instance, in a Wills or Trusts problem, having a diagram of the relationship between the parties can be of critical importance. In a Property problem (particularly one dealing with easements), having a physical drawing of the land and respective owners can help. Also, in a Secured Transactions problem, drawing a timeline of the different interests can prove useful for keeping things in order.

As you're reading, pay careful attention to the different parties involved. There is no more surefire way to lose points than by confusing parties and stating, "Anne gets the Rolls Royce," when you meant to say, "Brad gets the Rolls Royce," but just got confused. Those are lost points because you mixed up a name. Keep them straight in your head.

Focus on issue spotting as you read. Along the way of the fact pattern, there will be events and twists that lead to one legal consequence or another. They are embedded in the problem, and spotting them is key to your success. For instance, someone will either record a deed or they won't; someone will enter a home through a window that is already open; someone will visit a property and observe power lines running down the front yard, etc. All these events may seem subtle and somewhat meaningless, but you will come to learn (if you haven't already) that they each have significant legal consequences. You want to become an expert at spotting those issues. As you spot them, make a note in the margin about the applicable rule of law that relates.

For instance, if I read a problem that says, "Mary threw a softball at Frank as he was walking away from her," I may note in the margin, "No apprehension," to signal to myself that Frank did not see the softball coming; therefore, the "reasonable apprehension" element of an assault was not met. Whenever you spot an issue, there is almost always going to be an associated rule of law. Write it down as you see it.

e) Outline your answer

Find a space in your test booklet to make a quick outline for each sub-question. I usually draw vertical lines on my test booklet and create "columns" for each sub-question. Then I will make a quick bulleted list of the topics and areas I want to address in that answer. I do not spend a great deal of time detailing the answer in my outline. I simply write a bulleted list of things to touch on to serve as my guide.

Sometimes, when you outline your answer, you will not yet know your answer to the question being posed. That's ok. If you know the answer, include it in your outline; if you don't, simply write a "TBD" and worry about finding the answer as you analyze.

f) Write your answer

By this time, you should have a lot of notes on your page. You will have a plethora of rules of law that you have identified, and these form the foundation of your answer. Now it is time to get to work and start writing your answer.

1. First paragraph

Your first paragraph should contain: (1) a direct answer to the question and (2) a statement of the key issue. Your goal is to provide a clear and concise demonstration to the examiner that you know what you're talking about.

Using the example above, we might write, "No, Mary cannot be found liable for battery. The issue is whether or not battery can be committed when the plaintiff does not reasonably apprehend the defendant's act."

The examiner reading this can quickly get a sense for how on-track you are with the answer. First, they will know whether you have answered the direct question being asked. Second, they will know whether you answered it correctly (Yes/No). Third, they will know whether you have spotted the key issue upon which the answer hinges. Starting your answer on the right note is key, and it sets the stage for success.

Note that, sometimes when you begin writing, you may not know the answer to your question quite yet. If you do not know the answer, simply write a "TBD" where the "Yes" or "No" would be, and remember you will need to come back and edit this after your analysis.

2. Second paragraph

Your second paragraph should be familiar to you. In this paragraph, you are writing the applicable rule(s) of law. In many cases, there will be multiple rules. This is where you use your legal writing skills from law school. I will not attempt to explain how to write rules of law, as you already know that. Just suffice it to say that you are setting forth the applicable rules of law to set the stage for your analysis that will follow.

3. Third paragraph

As expected, your third paragraph is about applying the facts to the rule of law. Again, the intent of this short book is not to explain legal writing, as you already know that. Instead, I will offer a few suggestions.

The facts in the problem are, more often than not, there for a specific reason. Very rarely have I found that bar exam problems contain facts that are irrelevant in some fashion. As such, when you are applying facts to the law, constantly ask yourself whether you have used all the facts. If there are facts that you have not used, ask yourself why they may appear in the problem. Do they change the calculus on some particular analysis? Are they red herrings to lead you astray? Do you create a relationship or dependency you should consider? Think carefully about any "loose" facts and explicitly ask yourself whether they have meaning and should be used in your analysis.

There is another point of importance. There may be cases where you simply do not know the law, but you know a fact is important. I cannot speak to bar examiner scoring, but I can say, in numerous Barbri examples (which are supposed to be from actual bar examiner scoring), you can get points simply by stating the facts. For instance, if Harry fails to record his deed, but you have forgotten the details of a notice statute and the implications that creates, you should at least include a statement in your answer that says, "Harry failed to record the deed." This at least signifies to the bar examiner that you recognized this issue, and it has some bearing on the problem. As stated above, the facts are there for a reason, and something as important as the failure to record a deed (or some other fact of seeming importance to another area of law) is worth identifying in your answer simply to signify that you know it has some meaning, even if you don't know exactly what.

g.) Review your answer

After you have completed your answer, take a few moments to review it. If you did not know the answer in your first paragraph (per above), now is the time to erase that "TBD" and write a clear "Yes" or "No" statement. You should have finished your analysis and applied the facts to the law, and now you have a clear indicator of how the answer comes out.

Read your entire answer from start to finish. Make sure the statements are clear, it is easy to read, there are no grammar or punctuation issues, and you have covered the key facts and areas of law. Briefly put yourself in the shoes of the examiner and act like you are reading the answer with fresh eyes. How does it sound? Does it sound like someone who knows what they're talking about wrote this? Or does it sound like a smattered mess of gibberish? If the latter, you have some editing work to do at this point.

After you have read your answer, read the problem again. Did you catch all the issues? Did you touch on all key facts? Scan the notes you wrote when you first read the call of the question and the problem. See if you wrote anything that you did not include in your answer. On many occasions, I failed to do this and forgot to include something that initially jumped out at me. Take a few seconds to double-check yourself and make sure you didn't miss anything.

One final suggestion worth noting: if you have finished your answer but are unsure of one part of your answer, circle it on your test booklet or mark it somehow. You should signal to yourself that there is something here you want to come back to if you have time at the end of answering all your MEE questions. You should not spend more than 30 minutes on one problem, but you may find yourself with extra time once you have completed all the problems. If so, having an easy way to identify questionable areas of your answer will help focus your efforts to maximize results in the waning minutes of the MEE. Once you have reviewed and are satisfied, you're all done. Move on to the next one.

CONCLUSION

The MEE covers a broad swath of law and can be a daunting task for most test takers. The key to mastering the MEE is to practice, practice, practice. Through practicing problems, you will learn the black letter law and refine your process, so you can perform on test day.

1. Make an absolute goal of completing AT LEAST 60 practice MEE problems before your exam, ideally more.
2. View practice problems as a learning opportunity:
    a. Spend time understanding what you missed.
    b. Update your outlines and force yourself to type the missed answer.
    c. Create a separate "Outline of Missed Answers" to aggregate all your missed answers and force yourself to type them a second time.

d. Practice your approach to MEE questions:
e. Read the call of the question and glean valuable information.
f. Jot down key legal rules triggered by the call of the question.
g. Write out your headings.
h. Read the problem.
i. Spot and mark issues.
j. Keep relationships and key parties straight with a diagram.
k. Write your answer:
l. First paragraph – Yes/No answer and statement of issue
m. Second paragraph – Applicable legal rules
n. Third paragraph – Apply facts to rules

3. Review and polish your answer.

CHAPTER 5

Multistate Bar Examination (MBE)

1. Overview

In my opinion, the Multistate Bar Examination (MBE) is the most difficult component of the bar exam. As of the date of this writing, every state in the country, with the exception of Louisiana, administers the MBE. That said, the odds are good that you will need to learn the skills necessary to succeed on this test.

The MBE consists of 2 sessions of 3 hours

each in which examinees are required to answer 100 multiple choice questions per session. The math works out to 1 minute and 48 seconds per question. You may be thinking that sounds like a lot of time to pick one of four answers. You're wrong. It is not a lot of time on an MBE question. MBE questions are typically 2-5 paragraphs of information followed by the call of the question. In these 2-5 paragraphs, a plethora of facts and potential issues that you will need to sift through will be presented. Some subjects, such as Property or Contracts, tend to contain more information than others. The content of MBE questions is not something that can be easily skimmed to find the right answer. Generally, every word in the question carries meaning that could change the outcome of the problem.

Because of the depth and volume of questions, the MBE is exhausting. It is likely you have done little before in your life that will entail the sustained focus and concentration needed to do well on the MBE.

The only good news of the MBE is that the scope of potential topics is more limited than most MEE sections. Generally, you will only be asked to answer questions from among the following topics: Contracts, Torts, Real Property,

Civil Procedure, Constitutional Law, Criminal Law, Criminal Procedure, and Evidence. While those topic areas are more limited than the MEE, they still represent a broad swath of information you must learn and be able to extract from your memory and work with under timed conditions.

2. Practice, practice, practice

Once more, the best approach to MBE problems is to practice. As with the other parts of the bar exam, practicing MBE problems lets you hone your mind and body to this particular type of exam. It allows you to build your internal clock to start to recognize when 1 minute and 48 seconds has passed and you must move on. It helps you build the stamina and fortitude necessary to complete two sessions of 100 questions each.

My suggestion is that, at a bare minimum, you should complete 1,400 practice MBE questions before you take the exam. That is the low end of the threshold. I saw a survey on one of the law student forums where the vast majority of people had completed between 1,400 and 1,900 questions. Somewhere in that range is the sweet spot for preparing yourself for the exam. If you complete less than that, the odds are good that you will have missed certain issues and questions that may frequently arise on the bar exam. If you complete at least 1,400 practice questions, you will have exposed yourself to the vast majority of problem types you are likely to encounter, and you will have trained your body to handle the pressure of the MBE.

Your individual bar program may not require you to do that many questions. If not, I suggest you purchase a supplement, such as Adaptibar or one of the Emmanuel books, to provide you with additional questions.

Just like the other areas of the exam, you will want to do at least a few practice sessions that simulate the full scope of this portion of the exam. That means that, at least twice, you should spend 3 hours answering 100 questions. It goes without saying again that doing so will build your mental and physical stamina to handle the challenge on exam day.

3. Calibrate your internal clock

Building your internal clock for MBE questions is critical. The worst scenario you can face is to realize you are 1 hour into your first session and you have completed 20 questions. Panic will immediately set in, and you will then feel stressed and rushed to complete the remaining 80 questions. As mentioned, MBE questions require such intense concentration that any semblance of anxiety that clouds your mind is taking away your focus from the question. Rushing through questions under a cloud of anxiety and stress is a recipe for disaster. If you find yourself at that point, you have already lost. The key is to never get to that point. In order to avoid that point, you must build your internal clock.

I found that by completing so many practice questions, you will eventually learn when the timer is near 1 minute and 48 seconds and it is time to move on. Eventually, I found myself tuned to about 1 minute and 30 seconds for every question. My advice is to work through enough practice questions until you have internalized your timer and you can "feel" when it is time to move on. When you get to that point, move on to the next question. Some people may say it is alright to spend more time on some questions because you will make it up on others. I disagree with that advice. You simply do not know what questions lie ahead of you. If you hit a question that requires 2 minutes and 30 seconds and you spend that time, you do not know whether there are 10 more questions ahead that require over 2 minutes. You're gambling with your time and hoping the questions shake out to match the time you have left. My suggestion is to maintain control and stick to your time limit. Once you hit your internal clock, move on to the next question. We'll discuss below how and when to come back to questions if you have time left at the end.

4. Set small milestones for yourself

Part of the exhaustion from the MBE comes from intensely focusing for 3 straight hours. There is really no way around this. There is simply not enough time baked into the MBE for you to stand up, stretch, and take a break. I remember, in New York, we had to take the exam in a mammoth convention center, and the bathroom was about 200 yards away. I sat there during the MBE mentally calculating how long it would take me to get to the bathroom and back and how many questions I would fall behind in the process. In the end, I had to go (I had caught a cold the day before and direly needed to blow my nose, as my tissues had essentially dissolved), and in the process, it probably took me about 2 minutes, which equates to almost 3 questions worth of time. That is critical time, and you do not have the luxury to waste it on a break.

So what do you do to break the tedium? What I did was set interim milestones. For instance, I would tell myself that every 20 questions (which represents 1/5 of a session), I would take a small "break." This break was really nothing more than lifting my eyes from the paper, leaning back in my chair to stretch by back, and stretching my hands to keep my fingers limber. This literally afforded me a break of no more than 5-10 seconds, but when you are so intensely fixated on answering questions, having even this tiny semblance of a break to look forward to offered some solace that you would not have to concentrate for 3 hours straight and that you would be offered a momentary reprieve.

These mini-breaks also helped me keep the pace, for they allowed me to chew up chunks of 20 questions at a time and focus on those. Over the course of the session, those chunks of 20 questions obviously add up to 100, and then you are done.

Whatever you do, look for some way to break the tedium and reward yourself for your progress. For you, it may mean closing your eyes and meditating for 10 seconds. For others, it may mean staring at the ceiling. Do whatever works best for you, but see if building mini-breaks into your routine helps you in the long run.

5. Approach to the MBE

Your approach to the MBE is, in essence, an abbreviated version of your approach to the MEE. Since you have 1 minute and 48 seconds versus 30 minutes, you obviously will not follow all the same steps, but you will notice some familiarities.

a) Read call of the question and the answers

This is no different than the MEE. Immediately scan the call of the question and read what you are being asked to do. Just like with the MEE, this will give you valuable information on what the question is about, so you can focus your mind on the specific topic being tested.

The one additional step with the MBE is that you will also want to skim the answer choices. Skimming the answer choices will give you critical information on your potential options for answers. To some extent, understanding what choices you have to select from limits your scope of possible areas of the law to pursue as you read the full question and helps you focus more quickly. Don't spend time trying to choose the right answer; your goal is simply to calibrate your mind with what topic is being tested and what specific area within that topic you will be working with.

b) Write down rules that will be implicated (if appropriate)

Just like the MEE, you may want to jot down the rules of law that are implicated by the question. Again, I do not mean fully writing them out. I mean simply scratching out a mnemonic or a few notes to help you recall the rules and elements. A word of warning here – you have much less time to work with, and in many cases, you will not want to waste your time writing down rules of law. I would suggest, if you come across a question that is asking about a particular rule of law and that rule is complex or you believe you may have trouble recollecting it, write down some quick notes immediately to trigger your memory after you finish the fact pattern. For instance, I often had trouble remembering the rules for when a court's decision could be appealed before final judgment. If I came across a question of this nature, I might write down abbreviations for the rules for the Interlocutory Appeals Act and the Collateral Order Rule, as I tended to mix them up, and I wanted to get them down on paper before my mind got cluttered with a lot of facts from reading the problem. In instances like this, where you risk losing the rule of law in your mind amongst the noise of the problem, you may want to consider jotting down the rule to come back to it when you begin answering the question.

c) Read the question

Once you have read the call of the question and the possible choices (and possibly jotted down some rules of law), it is time to read the question. This part is pretty self-explanatory. Start from the beginning and read every sentence carefully, making sure you digest every word. I would often pause after each paragraph and do an internal check to make sure I had mentally processed everything I just read. There are fewer ways more certain to get questions wrong than by not understanding or acknowledging all the facts. Read quickly but thoroughly. Make sure you understand names, dates, locations, and any other critical information.

As with MEE questions, it is often helpful to draw diagrams to understand what is happening. Things can get confusing very quickly when a number of parties or pieces of property are involved. If diagramming helps, draw a quick sketch or family tree to make sure you have all the pieces mentally straight.

As you read through the questions, you will be issue spotting, like you did on the MEE. Look for issues where a certain fact or circumstance could change the outcome of the problem. These are critical and are imbedded in virtually any MBE question.

Most importantly, make sure you understand and identify the critical rules of law that come in to play with the facts you have been given. Any problem may implicate 1 or more rules of law. The answer to the question hinges on whether you have correctly identified and applied the rule of law. As you are reading, the issues and facts you come across should trigger your mind to identify these rules of law.

When you have finished reading the question, you should: (1) fully understand the story told, including characters, dates, and locations, (2) have identified key issues upon which the answer hinges, and (3) have identified the rule(s) of law that are implicated.

d) Answer the question in your head before looking again at the answers

This step is critical and, in my opinion, a key indicator of success. Once you have finished reading, DO NOT immediately scan back down to the answer choices. Pause for a moment and mentally state in your head what you believe the right answer is. You have read the problem, and as you read, you identified issues, and you identified the rule of law. You now have all the information you need to answer the question. In your head, determine what you believe the answer to be.

It is critical that you do this before you look at the answer choices. The answer choices invariably include red herrings that are designed to steer you mentally one way or the other. By deciding for yourself what the answer is, without being influenced by the red herrings, you are eliminating one of the primary tricks up the examiner's sleeve and taking away their power. I cannot quantify this, but I can tell you that, when I explicitly made a point to do this on practice MBE tests, my scores were significantly better than when I fell into the trap of looking for the answer amongst the choices versus deciding what it was on my own.

If you come up with an answer you are confident in choosing, look to the answer choices and see if your answer is there. If there is an answer that matches your answer, including outcome and rationale, you've probably found the right answer. However, you should not just immediately mark this answer and move on. Do the diligence of scanning the other answers to make sure nothing seems more appropriate. If nothing looks better than what you came up with on your own, mark it and move on.

e) Eliminate the wrong choices

Unfortunately, there will be many, many questions where you do not yet know the answer and cannot come up with it without looking at the choices. In these situations, you can look to the answer choices, but you should be methodical about your process.

SIMPLE STRATEGIES FOR THE BAR EXAM

Your first step should be to eliminate any answers that are obviously incorrect. You have four choices with every answer. If you can cross out 1 that is obviously wrong, you increase your odds of choosing the right answer to 33%. If you cross out 2, your odds are now 50%. In the long run, these odds add up and help you. There will be some answers you know are obviously wrong. Whether they misstate a rule of law, use facts incorrectly, or simply come to a conclusion that you know is wrong, you should be able to eliminate at least one choice. Your goal here is to whittle down the four choices to the smallest number of potential right answers as possible and then guess the best answer from that smaller pool.

Do not skip this step. Take an explicit action to draw a line through the letter of the choice you know is not correct. Doing this small act indicates progress and will build your confidence as you know you are shifting the odds in your favor. Mark out the wrong answers, look at what is left, select the best answer, and move on.

f) Mark questions that require further review

If you follow the method described above of setting your internal clock to 90 seconds per question, you will undoubtedly have to move on from questions when you do not feel good about the answer. The beauty of setting your internal clock to about 90 seconds is that you ensure: (1) you will answer every question, and (2) you will have rationed some time for review at the end.

Before we move on, I should state that it is paramount that you answer every single question. You do not get points deducted for missed answers, but you will leave points on the table if you do not at least take a guess at an answer. Tune your internal clock to allow you to answer every question.

So, your internal clock is telling you to move on, but you're not positive of the answer you picked. What then? This is where a personal marking system comes into play. Personally, I used a system of tagging questions with a 1, 2, or 3 as follows.

1. I feel pretty certain about this answer, but it wouldn't hurt to review once more.

2. I feel directionally correct, but still have significant doubts about my answer.

3. This question is incredibly complicated, and my answer is basically a guess.

After I finished each question, I would tag it with one of those numbers above the question and circle the number so it stands out. Obviously, if I was absolutely certain about an answer, I would simply not tag it with a number. There is no point reviewing those I was certain about.

Now, once you have finished completing all 100 questions, you should have some time left. If you have calibrated your internal clock to 90 seconds per question, you have 30 minutes left. However, things never worked out like that. Invariably, I would find myself with anywhere from 10-20 minutes left. This is solid review time. You can take solace in the fact that you have completed all 100 questions, and you will not leave any points behind for blank answers. Now, your task is to make the best use of that time.

There are some different ways you could approach this, but I will tell you the way I did. I would start with question #1 at the start of the booklet and look through the questions I had marked with numbers. For anything I had marked with a number 1 ("pretty certain"), I would spend a decent amount of time reviewing and ensuring I had the right answer. In my view, these are questions where you are so close to scoring points that you should spend the extra time solidifying those points on your score and making sure you get them. These are typically questions you understand and can easily digest, but you just want to make 100% certain you have not missed a nuance or misapplied the rule of law. I always looked to button up the number 1's.

If I came across a question marked number 2, I would also spend a decent amount of time on it to see if the second time around made the question any clearer in my mind. In doing this, however, I would perform triage. If I read the question again and it was not clearer or was still incredibly muddy, I would do my best to verify my answer or change to the correct answer without overanalyzing it. You can easily get bogged down in a complicated question and still miss it, when you could have spent that time scoring some easy points on other questions that can be more readily analyzed. Basically, for questions marked with a 2, take a second read and see if things are clearer on this second pass or if anything different sticks out. If you read the question again and everything is just as confusing as the first pass through, take your best guess and move on. Do not get bogged down.

If I came across a question marked 3, my strategy was similar, but I was more attuned to the need to move on. For me, questions involving mortgages and recording statutes often seemed to be marked with a 3. These questions can be full of facts and incredibly complicated. Sometimes, if I remembered that the question was complicated and I had no hope of coming to the right answer, I wouldn't even look at it a second time. If I thought I might be able to shed some new light on the answer, I would take a quick pass through it. A lot of this depends on how much time you have left and how you feel after glancing at the problem again. If there is no hope and you will just waste your time, just make sure you have marked it with your best guess and move on.

By tuning your internal clock to 90 seconds per question and using this numbering approach, you do several things. First, you ensure you answer all 200 questions. Second, you mitigate having to deal with constantly calculating how much time you have left and whether you are on track. If you tune your internal clock through practice and just keep moving through the questions, you do not have to worry so much about the clock. That is not to say you shouldn't do periodic checks of the clock to make sure you are following your internal timer, but they should be quick checks and not full, mental calculations of your progress and trajectory. Third, by following this approach, you are strategically using your time remaining to score points on questions you are most likely to get correct.

While you could easily spend 5 minutes on a complicated mortgage question and, in doing so, you may increase your odds of getting the right answer by 20%, that time is better spent reviewing 5 other questions that you are fairly certain about and making sure you nail those 5 points (or at least most of them).

Conclusion

The MBE is largely a test of mental fortitude. I dreaded the MBE day much more than the MPT/MEE day because it always felt so exhausting. The key to beating the MBE, as with the other areas, is to practice, hone your mind and body to the challenge, and develop your own personal system or process for answering these questions. If you do, you will likely succeed.

1. Practice, practice, practice by doing no less than 1,400 practice MBE questions, including at least 2 rounds of 100 questions each.
2. Calibrate your internal clock to about 90 seconds per question.
3. Set small milestones after every 20-25 questions, where you take a 5-10 second mental break to reward yourself.
4. Develop and refine your approach:
   a. Read the call of the question and the answer choices to identify the area of

law being tested and the specific topic within that area.

b. Read the question to spot key facts, issues, and rules of law implicated.

c. Draw diagrams to keep facts straight if you need to.

d. Answer the question in your head before you look through the choices.

e. If you do not know the answer, explicitly cross out choices you know are incorrect to increase your odds of selecting the right answer.

f. Answer the question as best as you can.

g. Mark the questions that you need to review by using some sort of system to designate degree of certainty for your answer.

h. h. Use the extra time you have left to review your answers strategically.

CHAPTER 6

The Actual Exam

You've finished studying; now comes the time to put it all together and find your way onto the pass list. As you settle in to the final days of exam preparation, keep your focus on the details and follow your plan through to completion.

1. Get settled in your hotel room early

If you have the luxury of staying at your own

apartment or house before the bar exam, you can skip this section. Assuming however that you're traveling to the bar exam, you should plan your trip so that you check into your hotel two days before the bar exam. Obviously, you could check in the day before, but that creates a lot of unnecessary risk. What if your flight is delayed? What if the reservation gets messed up and there is no room? What if your room isn't what you expected and you need to change rooms? What if you forgot something critical and need to find a store to buy it? Mitigate all these risks by checking into your hotel room two days before the exam. Doing so gives you time to acclimate to your environment and take care of any last minute issues that come up. Something is bound to come up, so play it safe and give yourself time. Your goal in these two days is to get all the logistics out of the way, so you can rest and focus, knowing you have eliminated every impediment humanly possible.

If you do nothing else upon checking in, be sure to check your computer. Your computer is your lifeblood, and if you have to handwrite your exam, you may be in trouble. Spend some time, once you get checked in, verifying that everything about your computer is properly functioning. Plug in the computer, turn it on, make sure it boots up, make sure you remember your password, and make sure you can log in to the testing software. If you have not taken the mock exam yet, do so now.

2. Prepare your meals

Eating before the bar exam is critical, and that includes not just the morning of the bar exam but the days and nights before. You want to make sure your body is getting sufficient food and energy to get you through the next few days. Now is not the time to experiment and try new things that may have unknown effects on your body. You want everything within your control now, and you do not want to worry about what your body is doing processing some strange food while you're trying to focus on the exam.

In South Dakota, I made the foolish mistake of eating two giant bean burritos the night before the bar exam. I was so exhausted from the flight and subsequent drive to the testing site that I was "rewarding myself" with a big meal. That was a mistake. Until I went to bed, I felt bloated and tired. I went to sleep worried that I would wake up and be at less than 100%. This was an unnecessary worry that didn't need to happen on the night before the exam.

Use your extra time before the exam to figure out where you can get good, solid, and healthy food. Find a grocery store and pick up what you plan to eat the morning of the exam and get it all prepped and laid out, so you don't have to worry about a thing when you wake up on the morning of Day One.

3. Double and triple check your "Allowed Items" list

The bar examiners will have provided you with an extensive list of items that are allowed and not allowed at the test site. You should have been checking this list before you ever traveled, but now is your last chance to do something about it if you are missing something or had planned to bring something that isn't allowed.

Pull out your list. Grab a pen or pencil. Go methodically down the list and make sure you have everything expected, and you are not planning on bringing anything on the prohibited list. Take everything you plan to bring and set it all together. Most bar locations seem to require everything brought in a quart-sized plastic bag. Now is the time to fill the bag and set it aside, so it is ready on test day morning. If you are missing something, find your local store and go get it. This is the reason you checked in on time.

Don't forget to check your laptop for any files or discs in the CD drive that you're not allowed to have. You don't want to get kicked out of the bar exam because of something you completely overlooked.

4. Conduct reconnaissance on the testing site

Use your extra time to scope out your test site. After verifying your laptop is functioning, this may be the next most important part of your last-minute preparation. You absolutely do not want to show up at the testing location for the very first time on test day. There are a multitude of issues that you can mitigate by visiting in advance. What if you get lost and can't find it? What if you have no idea where parking is? What if you don't know where the entrance is? What if the site is not at all what you envisioned or expected? What if it is too cold or too hot and you didn't dress appropriately?

By visiting the test site in advance, you mitigate many possible issues and pave the way for a lower stress morning on Day One. Locate the site, drive to it, drive around, look to see where the parking is, and find out where the entrance is. If you are able and allowed, get out of your car and walk inside. Find out where the testing hall is. Figure out which entrance you will go in, how you will walk there, and how long it will take. Take a peek inside and look at the seating arrangements. Are there hard chairs or soft chairs? What is the temperature like? Will you need to bring a sweater or extra jacket (if allowed)?

The vast majority of your fellow test takers will not visit the site in advance. By visiting in advance, you are already a leg up on them. You have mitigated pre-test jitters that they will be processing the morning of Day One. Instead of those jitters, you will be focusing on the first question of the day, as you already knew what to expect. You're already ahead of the game.

A word of caution – if your examiners have told you not to visit the site or to stay away, pay heed to their warning. The last thing you want is to get in trouble for poking around ahead of the exam. For all of the exams I have taken, there have been people setting up ahead of the exam. I never got in trouble but was always cautious enough to avoid being a disruption. Keep a respectful distance and keep moving but take in as much information as you possibly can about the test site the day before the exam. You will save yourself a lot of unnecessary worry on test day.

5. Deflect the nervous energy around you

When Day One comes, you will quickly notice the exam room and building are filled with an incredibly tangible, nervous energy. You can almost feel the buzz in the air. There are so many people grouped so closely together, who are all incredibly nervous about what is to come. Don't be one of those people. It is easy to get sucked into that nervous energy and to lose yourself in the moment. Avoiding that pitfall will put you a leg up on the other test takers.

If you have put in your study time, and you have prepared based on some of the methods described here, you have done far more than the average person. Trust in that. Trust that your level of preparation has exceeded the nervous buzz around you and find confidence in that. You have done countless practice problems – probably more than most of the people around you. You have drilled information into your head while you were at the gym, driving around, and in any free minute. Your dedication and commitment to your bar study has exceeded most everyone else's. You are better prepared than the people around you, and now is the time to savor that and find assurance and comfort in it.

At the end of the day, the bar exam is a competition. Your answers will be graded in comparison to those who take the test with you. While they buzz around, absorb yourself in the confidence that you are capable and prepared and have no need to be nervous. The only thing you need to do is execute. Cherish this feeling, walk through the nervous buzzing, take your seat, and prepare to do what you need to do. Let everyone else worry around you. That's not why you're here.

6. Don't study at lunch

When we took our lunch break on Day One of the New York bar exam, there were literally hundreds of people aimlessly attempting to cram outlines and flashcards into their brains. I couldn't help but think what a waste that was. If you do not know something by lunch break of Day One, you're in dire trouble. Lunch time is not the time to try to learn new information. You will do nothing more than cloud your mind with facts when you're already in an anxious frenzy. Instead, you should savor the hour you have. Get your lunch, sit down and eat, and relax. Go to the restroom and wash your face or freshen up. Use your time on something productive that will relax your mind and allow it to access the information you have stored there.

Trust in the knowledge that you know the material and have done the necessary preparation to succeed. Studying over lunch during the exam is counterproductive and should be avoided. Again, let the others buzz away with their nervous energy. You have reached the point where you simply do not need to study at lunch, so don't do it.

CHAPTER 7

Closure

I appreciate you taking the time to read to this book. I hope that, somewhere in the book, you have found some tips and advice that may be helpful for you. Again, this is not intended to be a step by step guide to passing the bar exam. What is offered here are simply the tips, habits, and practices that have served me well on three separate bar exams. Nothing in this book is a substitute for studying your bar preparation materials and understanding your specific juris-dictional requirements.

The overall mantra of my approach is to over-prepare and then enter the exam with a relaxed confidence based on your level of preparation. You want to enter the bar exam with more practice, information, and confidence than you need to pass the exam. Shoot well beyond your target, and you will likely succeed.

The bar exam is a tangible, understandable, and manageable exam. It is not something to be feared and dreaded. Do not listen to the people who tell horror stories about the bar exam or make themselves feel better by stirring the anxiety of others. If you prepare, none of that applies to you. By following your bar prep program, committing yourself to the exam, and enacting positive habits throughout your studies, you will succeed. I wish you the best of luck in your studies and hope your journey is fruitful and productive.

If I can be of any help at all, please feel free to email me through:

www.lomackpublishing.com

THANK YOU

Thank you for taking the time to read. If you found value in reading, please consider leaving a review wherever you purchased it from. Reviews will help others find this book.

Proceeds from the sale of this book support Lomack Publishing, a tiny self-publisher dedicated to promoting the rights, dignity, and interests of animals through thoughtful, self-published literature.

If you are interested in animal issues, please visit www.lomackpublishing.com for a free short story based on the events of "Chasing the Blue Sky," my novel about a homeless dog in search of his forever home.

ABOUT THE AUTHOR

WILL LOWREY is an attorney and animal rights advocate from Richmond, Virginia. He graduated summa cum laude in just 2.5 years, ranked #1 in his graduating class with a Juris Doctor from Vermont Law School. He also holds a Bachelor of Science from Virginia Commonwealth University. Will has taken and passed three consecutive bar exams and is considering a fourth.

After a successful, 20-year career in the corporate world as a process engineer and project manager, Will embarked on a more fulfilling endeavor and entered law school to pursue a career in animal law. For close to two decades, both before and after law school, Will has been actively involved in animal causes. His experiences include deployments to assist animals in disasters, the closure of roadside zoos, caring for animals from dog and cock fighting cases, community outreach for low income pet owners in areas ranging from urban neighborhoods to Native American reservations, animal rights protests, animal sheltering, public records campaigns against large institutions conducting animal research, and countless other adventures.

While Will has always been a casual writer of fiction, including short stories and poems, he recently discovered the world of self-publishing and was immediately engrossed. His first novel, "Chasing the Blue Sky," has been regularly featured in the Top 10 animal rights books on Amazon, received acclaim from numerous blogs and review sites, and was recently contracted for audiobook production. Will is also the author of the short non-fiction work, *"Words on a Killing"* through Lomack Publishing and the legal article *"We the Pit Bull: The Fate of Pit Bulls Under the United States Constitution"* published in the Lewis and Clark Animal Law Review Journal, Volume 24, Issue 2. While most of Will's writing focuses on animal issues, he has dabbled in other genres, writing *"The Tenebrous Mind,"* a collection of short horror stories and *"Simple Strategies for the Bar Exam,"* a non-fiction guide to taking (and hopefully passing) the bar exam.

To contact Will, please feel free to email him through:

www.lomackpublishing.com